THE JOURNEY INTO SELF UNDERSTANDING

Valerie Harper

BOOKS BY VALERIE HARPER

The Falcons Guard Collection
A Young Girl's Guide into a Self-Empowered Life
Finding Home
The Journey Into Self Understanding
Love & Strength
The Wounded Feminine
Love & Strength the Workbook
Creating Your Own Family
Falcons Guard the Foundation – Master Book

A Falcons Guard Collection

The Journey Into Self Understanding

How to Lead Yourself Into a Great Life

A Falcons Guard Book Collection

BOOK THREE OF EIGHT

Valerie Harper

A MOUNTAIN LOTUS PUBLICATION
SCOTTSDALE ARIZONA
2015

First U.S. Edition

Copyright © 2015 by Valerie Harper

ALL RIGHTS RESERVED

For information about permission to reproduce selections from this book, write to Permissions at mountainlotuspublications@gmail.com.

Library of Congress Catologin-in-Publication Data
Valerie Harper, date.

The Journey Into Self Understanding: book three in Falcons Guard Collection / Valerie Harper. / 1st U.S. ed.

India & Mexico

Printed in the United States of America

THE JOURNEY INTO SELF UNDERSTANDING

Valerie Harper

FALCONS GUARD

This book was independently written on behalf of Falcons Guard Center; an organization that promotes love and creativity. At Falcons Guard, they are dedicated to helping families gain more understanding in order to help their family systems function with more harmony. The Journey Into Self Understanding is a book designed for individuals who may not always have the self-reflection required for healthy development. It is intended to provide some form of perspective for understanding who they are and what they purpose of their journey is.

Please note that no person whatsoever is responsible for how you use this information including the publisher, author and anyone involved in the production of this book. Any and all suggestions made are intended for those of sound mind who take personal responsibility in choosing to consciously develop themselves into success. You can learn more about Falcons Guard classes by visiting www.FalconsGuardCenter.org.

Falcons Guard Center
Mesa, Arizona

Thank you for your purchase of this book.
Proceeds go to benefit the youth of
Falcons Guard Center.

Special Thanks to: Dave Mietus,
Marianne Ferrari, & Mary Moore.

This Falcons Guard Center book is independently written. The copyright is solely owned by the author. Falcons Guard Organization has obtained the legal right to use them as promotion for their non-profit organization. No person, school, organization or group of individuals has the right to use, redistribute, reproduce or claim ownership over the material in anyway. Teaching rights require written and notarized permission from the author and publisher. Anyone in violation of copyright infringement laws as outlined in Chapter 5 § 501 Sections 106 through 122 106A(a) are subject to penalties as outlined in section § 506 for copyright infringement and will incur penalties for profits and damages. For information as to how you may use this material or how you may obtain teaching rights, contact the publishing house at MountainLotusPublications.com and the author at ValerieHarperConsulting.com

For those who are lost and searching, Falcons Guard Centers help you find your way. For more information, visit www.falconsguardcenter.org

CONTENT

Foreward by Elizabeth Inganamort
17
Introduction
23
Respect
27
Emotional Isolation
34
Personality
42
Conflict
50
Values
62
Family Roles
64
Behavior As Defense
86
Intuition
90
Conclusion
100
Workbook Section 1 – Leading Yourself Into a Great Life
104
Workbook Section 2 – Life Assessments
142
Workbook Notes for EQ Lessons 1-10
164
About the Author
192

"My philosophy is to mentor, nurture and instill into each child, values, self-respect, leadership skills and to encourage them to set an example that others will recognize and want to emulate."

Elizabeth Inganamort
Visionary & Founder of Falcons Guard Center

Foreward

My name is Elizabeth Inganamort and I am the founder and visionary of Falcons Guard Center www.falconguradcenter.org. I grew up as the oldest of eight children on a ranch in Sonora, Mexico. I came from a life where we didn't have electricity, plumbing, television or even a phone. I slept on a dirt floor. When it was unbearably hot inside the mud and brick house we had to sleep outside on the ground. We only had the life my parents provided us. In my own inner self I was a survivor and I knew I was different. I saw my mother being pregnant every year and I was shocked to think that was the life I was going to have to look forward to.

I wanted more, so I asked my father if I could go to school in the town that was 15 miles away by car. There was no school bus to take me every day so I had to leave my family and stay in the town during the week. I was only 6 years old when I started at the catholic school. I lived at the school with the nuns and other children. It was very hard and I suffered from being separated from my parents. When I was 14 I moved in with friends from school who lived in the town and they gave me a home, a bed and food. I got pregnant at age 17. I was scared and didn't know what to do but my father told me to deal with the circumstances. One of the reasons I ended up pregnant was because my parents never discussed with me how you can get pregnant. Here I was in my youth, when I am supposed to be in school learning, and now I'm dealing with a baby and the biggest responsibility of life. All of a sudden I was a single mom with no work and all alone and I had to grow up fast.

The author of this book, Valerie Harper, wrote a book on parenting and I loved it so much that I wanted her to do a book on teens. I would like for every teen to have a copy of this book and use it as a guide and personal counselor. I wish I had a book like this when I was a teen. This book answers many questions that teens might be afraid to ask and will get their mind thinking. When they read it, they will know they are not alone and that there are many other teens that have the same questions and issues. In this book they will see keys and advice on how to deal with different situations. Some are my own inspiration. Every teen should use this teen book as their best friend that they can trust.

My life is dedicated to all the youth that are facing tough situations and or alone on the street. The youth are my passion, my life. I have had to live through some tough situations but I had hope and my friends were there to help. Good friends and family will be there for you to help you know what is right and what is wrong. I came from a loving family but many teens do not and are alone. If you don't have a family or friends, know I'm that friend and that you have Falcons as a resource.

The teens are my inspiration and I can feel their desperation. I felt that way before in my life and I want to help. I would like the teens to respect their parents and to respect and value themselves to fight for their dreams. They need to have dreams and never stop learning.

My vision is to create a center for homeless and troubled teens and to nurture them and turn them into leaders. At the center they will learn respect, values and responsibility. Until the Foundation raises enough money to build the center we are providing parenting classes and teen classes. I encourage any teen that wants to be involved to contact Falcons. If you want to be a leader or if you want to be an example or if you just want to help, there is always a place for you.

I not only help teens but also promote good parenting skills and advice. I want all the parents to have the best relationship with their children and for them to respect their children and let them be free. Parents need to discipline their kids, however encourage them and let them follow their heart and make their own life. You don't have time to love your children if you are always disciplining them so for each and every time you discipline, give the back five times in encouragement. Children need all the attention and love you can give them. The world is a scary place.

One of the best way for adults to help is to be a mentor to a teen. Teens need examples and sometimes they can relate to an adult that is not their parent. Show a teen that you love them. Show them respect and treat them as you would want to be treated. Remember that you should lead by example. Showing a teen love and kindness will also set an example for them to do the same when they reach adulthood.

Your donations, whether its money of time you are always welcome and help take teens off the street or provide them with food, clothing and education. I believe that everyone needs to love and respect each other not, only your family and friends, but strangers and well. There are many youth that don't have families to learn from or parents to teach them lessons and about life. Don't be selfish, give of yourself for the good of the world. The children are the future and need help now more than ever. Decide what it is you want to leave behind as your legacy and then work towards it.

Several years ago, I had the opportunity to take in a troubled teen into my house. I became her guardian and enrolled her in school. I helped her by giving her attention, love and encouragement. After she turned 18 she moved to Mexico. I am hopeful that one day when she is an adult she will do the same someone in need like I did for her.

I am personally mentoring other teens who came here from Mexico. One of them is now in college on a scholarship. I find great joy from giving myself to others.

Please use the book as a guide and resource and for answers to you questions. Valerie has excellent advice and knowledge that every teen needs.

Last but not least, I want to dedicate my knowledge for this work to my own boys Jorge, Willie and Jake. I also want to thank my own parents because they passed on to me all they learned from their parents. I have learned over time to appreciate that what they passed on to me and my brothers and sisters were important and valuable lessons. So again thanks to them and especially my father.

May God keep your light shining to deal with anything you are going through.

Besos,
Elizabeth Inganamort

Introduction

Your psychological responsibility as a teen is to prepare for adulthood. This book can be a guide to help you discover your truth from within so that you can be prepared for a fulfilling lifetime. You will not find a bunch of specifics about how you *should* live your life. Rather, you will be guided to understand yourself in a deeper way that when you operate from this truer self, you will naturally be inspired to live your life differently.

Grasping the concept of a self that is your ultimate Self can only be done by taking the journey inward. You have to know who you are in contrast to this place you are in to know that you are something so much greater than who you think you are.

The concepts in this book that are being introduced come from a psychological philosophy that if you use your creative talent and combine it with personal power, then you will be able to achieve your highest state of your true self, naturally. This doesn't mean that all will come easily. Everything in life is a process and journey. Life is naturally challenging for a reason. You are here to grow into the person you know you can be. This is a process.

Right now, you might have your own unique set of challenges to overcome. These challenges may have to do with self-esteem, friendships, sibling rivalry or your own parents not getting along. How you navigate any of these relationships will determine the success of your outcomes. This book is intended to assist you in navigating life more effectively by giving you some perspective as to how you operate internally.

Relationships are the very foundation for quality of life. When your relationships are not working, nothing feels right. When the relationship you have with yourself is conflicted, life will feel very difficult.

The reason why certain children and youth struggle into adulthood is because they never developed a healthy relationship with their true self. How you manage your relationship with the inner you will depend on how the people around you do. This book isn't trying to change you. It isn't going to tell you what is wrong with you or that you are bad. It is intended to inspire you to be the best you by helping you understand why you behave the way you do and hopefully inspire you to self-correct.

It is probably safe to assume that no matter what your age, you probably have a lot of questions about life. They may range from. "How do I make money?" "What am I supposed to do in this life?" "What is the purpose of this challenge?" all the way to "Why can't I get this right?" All the questions you have about what is right for your life can be found through higher thinking and feeling. This means when you use your mind, you use your intuition and you use the knowledge that other people have discovered to further your own mission, you can successfully lead yourself into a great life.

This book will assist you in developing the understanding that will all you to hold your inner power in such a way that you can create the life you want. This is the power that comes through self-understanding. Again, it is not a *How To* book in the sense that it will tell you what to say to your boyfriend or girlfriend if you have a fight. It will instead give you a framework from which to begin to operate from in life.

The benefit of having such knowledge is it will leave you feeling lighter, happier and freer. You will gain the support of your authentic nature and be able to flourish. Again, not all challenges in life are easy. Life will naturally force you to learn certain lessons. When life presents a challenge, move through it with a certain sense of ease knowing all will be taken care of by doing the right thing.

The benefits that come from knowing the real you is the real you always knows what to do. In the moment of facing the decision it just comes to you. You can rely on other people's input to tell you what to do and which way to go. But this isn't always helpful. Everyone has a different set of circumstances their advice doesn't always align to what you need to know. Taking the journey within to understanding your true self is what will give you your truth.

Your true self is always wise. You can think of your knowledge in a multi-dimensional way. You can think about what you know. You can think about what you know you don't know. You can think about what you don't know you don't know. And you can know about what you think you know. The combination of what you know and don't know is what gives you the quest for answers you seek in life. What we don't always know is that answers we thought we had could be incorrect. This is why all information must always be filtered through the *true self*.

As you read this, you may contemplate your own unique set of challenges that you are working through. You might feel overwhelmed with all of the challenges and limited resources you have to create the life you want. Whatever challenge you are facing, it doesn't have to be difficult. When you have the power of your real self, you can face anything and know life has you. This is because you have your *true self* navigating your life.

Wherever you are in life, no matter what challenge you might face, this book will give you the framework for understanding some of the basic functions of yourself. In understanding these aspects you a natural result will be how you hold your inner power so that you can create the life you want. Use this information to further propel you into a life of happiness, sense of adequacy and abundance. You are going to lead the next generation into its balanced state of personal harmony. Make the most of your personal journey through personal self-discovery.

THE JOURNEY INTO SELF UNDERSTANDING

Valerie Harper

1

Respect

To honor something or someone for who they really are means to respect them. When you respect yourself it means you have come to know who you are in such a way where you honor who you are without exceptions. It means you do not punish yourself by withholding, berating or subjecting yourself to things that are unloving just because you don't feel good about yourself. Self-respect comes from knowing who you are and honoring it.

With respect we have all things. We have love that is sustaining. We have a self that is self-preserving. With respect we have kindness. Respect what has real value. Respecting anything less than what holds value will lead you down a path of hardship. Respecting yourself means you care about your life. You care about your feelings. You care about who you are and are willing to learn how to set boundaries with the world around you so you can be self-protecting. Respect also means that you honor the people around you. This type of behavior is will be what leads your life to greater value.

You may have anger at your own parents, or fear from having had your caretakers abandoned you. You may have a lot of pent up rage at how people did or didn't treat you. You may feel lost and confused and don't know what to do. This anger is normal. When we lose respect we feel these types of things. However, the true self knows how to transmute any challenge into something for learning. It never leaves its place of self-respect. It maintains its values and acts from where it is at. There are a hundred different opportunities for violations to occur. Build the home of the true self within and you will be safe knowing you are in the part of yourself that was intended to nurture you.

....

Everyone is looking for freedom. We all want to feel good as individuals and be respected. When we feel respected we feel counted in. We feel included. This consideration we get from other people soothes our nervous system. We relax and are able to create because we feel safe.

When we feel disrespected we feel separated. We don't have the courage we would normally feel in order to participate. Many people feel disrespected. They feel their real self has been unheard. When this anger rises, it creates a real problem. The anger is a natural result of feeling forgotten. How people use anger determines whether or not it is destructive.

Exclusion in life occurs when people feel separated from the rest of life. Everyone perceives what is happening in life differently. What we perceive but do not feel invited to do can give us that feeling. There are a lot of things that make us feel separate.

As kids we are typically taught what *not* to do rather than what *to do*. When we live with too many rules that restrict us, it can separate us from what the rest of life is doing. We end up feeling depressed and uneasy. We can become uncertain as to how to assert our energy. When we are led by what we *shouldn't be doing,* it seems we always end up doing something *wrong*. This puts us in an uneasy state if this happens all the time. As a result we become stifled in creativity. Our fear of expression has us uneasy. A lot of things happen that cause us to close off to the internal self because we become more externally focused rather than inwardly listening.

It is important to live by values rather than a long list of what you *shouldn't do*. Values are easier to remember because they come from the real you. Long lists of rules of what you should or shouldn't do are overwhelming for the mind. Sometimes they are necessary as long as they are broken down into *why*. An undeveloped self that doesn't know *why* will not retain the commands of right and wrong. It won't make sense to them.

You want to listen to your inner self because it will give you answers. Listening to your inner self leads you to joy. Your inner self is your true self. It can be very conflicted when it receives so much guidance that is conflicting from the *outside*. Remember the conceptual image of what you don't know you don't know; what you think you know but is wrong and usually; what you know that is correct and what you don't know but can still tap into through the right knowledge.

Information is available to you to help you navigate life. The lack of information gives way to fear, restriction and sources outside of you ruling you. You need external guidance as long as it honors the *real you*. The rebellious, out of control side may need someone to control you. Rules are in place to keep people safe. Sometimes these rules are in place to keep yourself safe. There are too many variables to accurately state the overarching concept accurately. However, with self-responsibility comes great freedom.

Assume as much of your own responsibility as you can so you can let go of any feelings of self-restriction. To blame someone else renders yourself weak. This doesn't mean that everyone behaves perfectly. There are many intelligent people who operate without emotional intelligence and behave inappropriately. Even adults that seem to know a lot can make poor decisions and disrupt other people's lives greatly.

What assuming responsibility means is come from a place of respect for yourself and for others and half of your problems will disappear. If you find you cannot respect another person because of what they have done to you, you can always respect the lesson that they brought to you.

There is always an opportunity for respect and love. It may not be there right away. You may have to go in and find it within yourself. Rules can be eliminated by operating from good moral values. The more people develop a greater respect for life and for others, the less rules will be needed to be enforced.

2

Emotional Isolation

When we don't feel like we fit in to life's mold of what we think we "should" be, we can begin to feel separate from the world. The number one reason why people feel separate from the world is because we feel isolated or rejected. This feeling comes from closing off to parts of themselves because they feel unlovable.

Closing off to parts of the true self come from either not having enough positive interaction with other people for those aspects to develop. Or, the individual themselves has chosen to close down these parts of themselves for fear that these qualities make them unlovable. As a result of this occurring, people close off to their deeper self. This gives way to the sense that we are separate.

When we feel separate from the world, many things begin to happen. We suffer in our health because of the stress and anxiety separation places on our nervous system. We suffer in our minds because it doesn't receive enough intellectual stimulation. We can suffer in our finances because we must be connected in order for healthy financial circulation. And we suffer because the human spirit requires connection. We have to learn to reconnect to these aspects of our personality and inner most self in order to remedy these feelings of isolation and loneliness.

Parts of us don't properly develop until we experience positive interactions. However, with all of these reasons to seek good connection, there is still a good reason why people avoid it. People avoid connection because they have been conditioned to avoid intimacy. Intimacy has been said before as: in-to-me-see. We don't open up to intimacy if we are afraid of what people will see. Either it is too painful or intimidating, or it just wasn't developed so there is no understanding.

In order for any relationship to work, we must feel we are being *received*. Many families' social etiquette is lacking in this area of interacting. In some households, it is common to put down or sarcastically cajole other members, sometimes to no end without really considering other people's true feelings.

As children, we must form healthy bonds to someone in order to develop a healthy ability to relate with others and *be received*. Some people were born to angry, volatile, depressed, manic, fearful or emotionally disconnected parents making it extra difficult to know how to behave in ways that lead to greater intimacy. No matter what, the parents they were born unto had too small of a developed sense of self to adequately *receive them,* and as a result the children grew up feeling emotionally or physically abandoned.

Abandonment is the opposite feeling of being *received.* The terminology that can also describe this concept is rejected, denied, ridiculed, manipulated, hurt, sabotaged, betrayed, etc. Having parents or caregivers that reject, deny, deceive or minimize is due to their own unhealthy relationship with their true self, but also leads to a model that causes you to disconnect from *you.*

Anytime we are rejected or denied it causes us to separate from our true self. Experiences like this can cause us to separate so much from our truth of who we are that it causes us to select relationships that act out this same minimizing behavior as our caregivers. How your self was treated will impact the relationships you choose. Since relationships are the core quality that affects our lives, it makes sense why people who come from families who rejected or denied them emotionally have more challenges socially. This doesn't make these troubled people any less valuable. They just have more work to do to reconnecting to their inner selves in order to connect to that value, that *real* inner value.

When we come from a healthy model of intimate connection that is appropriate and loving, it will usually cause us to seek out other healthy connections. When we seek our radically unhealthy connections it is because we are attempting to heal what has been damaged. We feel safe in what is familiar. When we grew up in an environment that was so called emotionally unhealthy, then being around emotionally unhealthy people will feel safer to a certain part of the self because it is familiar. If dysfunction, rejection and denial is what has been familiar, it will be an easy selection unless we do something to correct it.

The Journey Into Self Understanding is important because it gives us an opportunity to see ourselves in a way we haven't seen ourselves before. Many people are operating unconsciously and don't even know it. They select relationships that are familiar believing they are *safer*. But in actuality, these relationships perceived as "safe" because they are familiar are often times the most damaging. They keep us sad, depressed and lonely. They may even sabotage our success and eventually the dysfunction in them eats up everything. It is very important to seek out healthy sources for support when this happens. And to strengthen yourself with your own healing so this cycle doesn't continue to happen.

………..

Whatever the reason is someone comes into our lives, we usually attract people who are going to bring us an experience that will show us more about life. We often seek those with radically similar or extreme opposite dispositions. To overcome a natural propensity to be drawn to something, we must see what it is there to teach us before we can release it. It is to recognize you always have a choice as to who you do and don't allow into your most intimate circle.

Whatever we obsessively seek in a relationship has something to do with the love we needed but didn't get. No matter the reason, the soul still knows what it wants. Whatever we suppress or deny has to do with the love we couldn't access. We learned to suppress or deny what we felt deprived of and so as a young adult this quality in a relationship may feel particularly hard to access.

Healthy connections are sought when healthy relationships are modelled for us. We are all creatures of habit. We look to what is emotionally and mentally familiar to us. We look to people and things to take care of us. We look for things that we perceive as *safe*. Even if they hurt us or don't help us out, we gravitate towards what is emotionally and physically familiar to us. This is all part of how and why we form relationships.

The relationships you form in your life will become the entire foundation from which you create your life from. Your friends and acquaintances will be your secured networking of people you derive pleasure from. The social interactions and networks are going to connect you to specific people and things. Having the kind of quality people in your life supports positive life experiences.

It is important to select the close relationships you have as there are many people who do not have everyone's best intention. Some do. Some don't. It depends on whether or not they are emotionally wounded. It also depends on how they manage their feelings from painful experiences. Many people would never hurt another but take out their rage with self-destruction.

Always trust your intuition when allowing a person to come into your close sphere of influence. Always act with the highest and good intentions of others while paying attention to your own needs that you have. Trust your gut intuition and work to maintain the best connections for as long as you can. The best rule of thumb is to always love and honor everyone but set healthy boundaries with all of them.

....

The personality is the part of yourself that is unique. There is no one quite like you. Nor does anyone have your exact same complexity. There are a lot of variations that make up your personality. Your personality is who you are no matter how you were raised. There is a certain disposition you have before any certain behavioral characteristics set in.

Behavior is slightly different than personality. You can have something bugging you and have it affect your personality. Ultimately, when you are emotionally free of stress, this is when you access your personality best. Behaviors are formed as a result of certain emotional patterns that were present.

No matter how you were raised, certain characteristics are innate. The tendencies of who you are were formed before you were born some believe. If you had a family that embraced these qualities then you felt accepted and loved. If you had a family that didn't accept these qualities you may not have felt embraced or even loved.

The psychological sensations of feeling rejected for who you are creates the feelings of you wanting to reject yourself for being the way you are. For some reason, in the mind, there is a perception that in doing so it will make you more loveable. This self-rejection can become a part of group survival. With the thinking being that if the rest of the group rejects you then there must be something wrong.

3
Personality

To love yourself means to embrace who you are. But first you must know *who* you are. You have many facets to you but we are going to begin with your personality. Personality assessments as follows are based on the psychology of the enneagram. An enneagram is a geometrical shape that maps the force of the soul's connection to the self and the world around it based on certain personality characteristics. Each one of us has each characteristic within us. It is just that we are more predominant with one in faces of conflict.

The following is a list of main personality characteristics. We all have a makeup of each one. How we develop it depends on the environment we are in. Our environment determines which aspect we can develop with most ease. Some environments only support peacemaking while frowning on achievement if the pursuit doesn't support other people within the surroundings. All environments and personalities are different. Understanding the main personality characteristics can helps align your thinking to your true personality characteristics.

The Personality Traits

The Perfectionist has a clear way of doing things. They tend to be hard on themselves as a way of demanding reality to be what they want it to be. They can take on more responsibility than their fair share because they want things to work accurately. They can easily feel judged or let down by others because this need can create rifts in interactions. They don't always know how they are turning people off in their conveyance of ideas.

When you are the Perfectionist, you feel driven by the need to feel in control by making their outer world match your inner concepts. You are most likely a great thinker. But when your intensity does not match the intensity of others you can easily be perceived as a controller. It is important to control the things you can without controlling others. When you are the Perfectionist, you can feel rejected if people turn away and decide they don't *need you*. This can be hurtful because in your mind, all you are really trying to do is make the world a better, more perfect, place around you.

As the Perfectionist type, it is important to recognize that you can be the person who gets the most things done. Understand this about yourself and when expectations are not being met around you, learn to kindly ask for what you want. If you make peace with the fact that nothing is ever really completed, you can actually attain the sense of accomplishment. The biggest hindrance to the Perfectionist is realizing perfection in nothing being perfect.

The Helper is someone who always helps out. When you're the helper you perceive yourself as feeling most wanted. But sometimes helpful personality types can feel used if people only go to them when they need something. If your predominant personality style is the helping type, it can feel difficult to say "no". Other people's opinions become too important and you are no longer doing what you need. The feelings of defeat come from not feeling like you get back what others people receive.

The confusion people seem to have with the Helper is that they are genuinely good people. Not everyone can relate to them though. The Helper may by at the receiving end of judgments and opinions. They can be perceived as weak, gullible or easy prey for takers. They can end up debasing their value by giving to the wrong, exploitive person. What is a gift can always be in a situation where it turns into a weakness.

The weakness the Helper has to look out for is the unconscious manipulative expectations of helping people and expecting something in return. While it is disappointing to be the Helper and not have it reciprocated, it is important for the Helper to learn good self care and find the balance. If they expect something in return for doing something for someone they have to say it. They can't just expect it. If you find you are the Helper it is important to practice using this energy to help yourself. Speak up for what you need. Ask for what you want. You love giving to the world yet if you give without anything coming back, eventually deplete yourself so you can't be of service the way you want.

The Achiever is a driven to accomplish whatever it is they perceive as a challenge based on their own moral compass. The achiever must do their best. They enjoy working and surmounting the challenge. They can feel exhausted from being driven to success. If you have the achiever personality type leading your way, the biggest challenge you will internally face is what happens when things *don't* go the way you had hoped they would. You might feel at a loss, insignificant or very low in self-worth. Your biggest downfall in your mind becomes the loss of status. This type of consciousness can create a lot of internal conflicts.

The most important thing you can do when you are the Achiever is recognize your need for recognition and accept not everyone is going to be able to give it. When times occur that you don't get the recognition you need, it is important to give yourself your own praise by giving yourself value just for trying.

The Individualist is the quiet person within the group that is highly self-aware. They don't always convey this knowledge or participate in what is taking place right then and there. They mostly observe others in order to avoid power plays of control. The Individualist can be highly judgmental of others in their silence. Or, they can just be silent in their observations without judging anything. They just like to observe how things work.

When you are the Individualist, it will be challenging to get yourself to engage with the rest of the group. Your individual self can be internally consumed with your problem solving and you can forget to let go, have fun and bring yourself in participation with others. If you ever wonder why you feel left out at times, it is important to know this is part of your personality type. Your feeling left out has less to do with others and more to do with how your mind works. This individual sense of self awareness is the motivating factor as to why you don't always participate. The key is to practice getting out of yourself regularly and letting yourself practice interacting with others in new ways.

The Observer is filled with brainpower to think, explore ideas. They need time alone to explore their thoughts. They are constantly dealing with their thoughts about the world so sometimes they appear removed from relationships. If your personality is in observation mode most of the time, your biggest challenge is learning how to let go of your thoughts and just participate in the moment of life without having to think everything through. The mind can become overactive when there is no one there to soothe you.

As the Observer, you love to think. You make a great writer or intellectual creativity. You feel most balanced when your thoughts achieve something. Once you make sense of everything, let it go and have fun doing nothing. This will help you make sense out of your inner world you are developing.

The Problem Solver is committed to solving problems. They often times have this compelling need to find the truth. They have to be right in the sense that if they are not aligned to the correct way, then they feel tremendous stress. These personalities do not like to make mistakes. They do whatever they can to make sure they get it *right*.

If you are the Problem Solver type, you might feel afraid to make the wrong decision. As a result, you may find yourself remaining stuck in a problem. Rather than just letting it go, you remain fixated on the solution. While you come up with the answers, these periods of problem solving can be highly stressful and even addictive. Thinkers like this can ruminate in their minds and feel like are accomplishing great feats while outsiders observe them as doing nothing.

If you are the Problem Solver, it is important to recognize and when you are creating more problems by dwelling on the problems in attempt to solve them. It is also important to remain connected to your health, your environment and relationships. If you find yourself slipping away into thoughts that prevent you from caring for your looks, environment or relationships, recognize it as a sign you are creating more problems by attempting to solve what ou are solving. You will find most of your success is in learning to be self-accepting.

The Visionary is someone who must be productive with their creativity and thoughts. They need to produce their ideas from invisible thoughts to the tangible physical. They must have a solid sense of direction with what they are creating. They have trouble get others on board with their vision because other people cannot always envision the outcome the visionary is internally seeing. Details can bog a visionary down. They can have so many ideas that they never have enough time for anything else. Like the mad scientist, if they can't get to where they want to be, to the outsider they may look a little intense or crazy. This is the energy of having a purpose as part of their destiny. The best thing they can do is relax, recollect their energies and move forward creatively; over and over again, as they create what they are envisioning.

The Take Charge Personality can appear to assume excessive control. However, like the Individualist who separates from the group, one must ask why this person is taking charge? Is it to control out of malicious intent? Or, is it to support the other person when they don't have the skills to support themselves?

The most effective take charge personalities are the ones who have taken the time to develop strong leadership. They allow for the individual will of others and yet they have that force of power when something needs correction.

Many people respond differently to these types of personalities depending on their individual relationship to authority. It can be extremely difficult being close to these types of people because they are always leading everything. It is frustrating for the take charge personality when no one is participating although they are highly individualistic in their personal responsibility. They have to work hard to feel satisfied with what they have gotten.

The Peacemaker is someone who works to avoid conflict at all cost. They can easily suppress their own feelings as to not raise a problem. They can be clueless about what they want. They allow themselves to be mistreated and even abused in order to avoid the problem. Their main objective of the Peacemaker is to be well-liked and have *everyone* get along. However, in the face of the people who prefer conflict, they can become a target. Everything can be very passive with them so they can easily be forgotten and or misunderstood.

If you are the Peacemaker, your need for peace can make people who have do not have the same need abusive towards you. To them, you are, or might be perceived as invalidating the injustice in them. People who are angry don't feel validated unless they see a similar energy of anger rise up in another person associate. It relieves the pressure within them because they feel supported. This can be a very difficult quality to understand to the peacemaker if they don't validate the other person's conflict.

If you are the Peacemaker type, it is important to recognize your natural tendencies to this role and pick your conflicts to bring peace to, wisely. Some conflicts run so deep that you can spend a lot of energy fixing something that isn't ready to heal or work amiably. Just like people who are angry need others to feel the anger of injustice with them, if you are a peacemaker, you need other peacemakers to support you, too. Making peace with things not being *at peace* will help you feel more successful at what you do; resolving conflicts and helping people see the lighter side of life again after what they have been through.

THE JOURNEY INTO SELF UNDERSTANDING

Valerie Harper

4
Conflict

Relational conflicts can easily arise in others and frequently do when people are not considerate of others. When people take the time to realize there are many people on this earth having an experience. We are all responsible for caring for ourselves and others. Understanding conflict is very important. When you come to the truth you can solve any problem. A conflict is nothing more than unresolved pieces of personal and collective truth that has yet to be fully and consciously identified.

Things you can do to move forward in a conflict is to understand what part of your personality is preventing from moving. Sometimes this means we have to step back and away from the conflict to gain understand as to what is really happening. As you gain perspective you can move forward with ease. The real concept of conflict resolution is seeing all personalities and how they are operating.

Some unhealthy ways people resolve conflict is to angrily take the other person to court, incessantly bully or intimidate the person they are annoyed with. Some people can spend hours talking about the problem. Other people can financially sabotage another by taking away their means of work or actually stealing money from them. Others can defend their position and explain why they are acting this way. They can argue and manipulate and do something bad to them if they don't adhere the suggested ultimatums. Or, people can just run away. But so any of these really resolve the core conflict? No, they don't. Either avoiding or initiating more conflict just creates a bigger conflict.

Conflicts among the personalities are resolved when people are willing to look at themselves and how they are responsible for what happened. Also, the empowered self will always turn a denial of obligation or duty and make themselves stronger from the abdication of someone else's responsibility. When people choose to negate responsibility, they turn down self-growth. The person within a conflict who refuses to look at themselves is the one who misses out.

Whatever method people who do not know how to resolve conflict use, it is important for *you* to find a set of alternatives that really work. For conflict resolution to work it has to produce a harmonious affect within the self that is not induced by denial, violence or through taking away something from someone else. True conflict resolution is in the genuine feeling or statement, "I have gained so much power from this lesson that nothing can affect me because I am a whole person." While it is painful to go through certain lessons, you can handle anything when you have your true self connected.

When solving any conflict, ask questions. You can work to understand the real problem. You can ask yourself how you might behave differently in order to get a better result? You may also wish to heal yourself of behaviors that are self-sabotaging when relating to others. You may recognize that this conflict is not about the other person but rather it may be something from within you. Or, you may see that the real conflict has nothing to do with you. They are using you as an outlet for what they emotionally do not have the strength to work through without abusing you. The real conflict may have nothing to do with you but you have to solve it on your end because somehow you got involved. All of these things are possibilities when working to solve conflicting energies. You know you have achieved real conflict resolution when the conflict no longer bothers you.

A conflict is nothing more than a disagreement in something. It is two or more parts working against the whole system that is functioning. You move into a dysfunctional system and you get kicked around because even in a dysfunctional system there is order, even if that order does not honor the true self or have respect for what is life giving. The order comes from anyone who operates under any particular set of rules. When your rules don't match up, there will be conflict. Unless the personality types can work together and see how they operate. Each personality type is fulfilling a function. If all personality types allowed for each one to function in their true nature, there would most likely be no more wards because there would be no more conflict within our nature.

At the heart of any external conflict is a conflict taking place within yourself. If the way you are doesn't fit with the rest of the crowd, you may begin to reject and deny certain aspects of yourself. Then there are times when you can't do anything about the conflict because the solution isn't yours to correct. It is someone else's. Someone else isn't taking responsibility and it is creating the wave of conflict in your reality. Conflicts are complex systems found within nature. When there is a disruption the urge is always to blame. However, the wisest choice is to become part of the solution instead of the problem.

Some conflicts grow to be so big that people have no clue how they actually started. All they know is that there is a complexity of involvements. They know who they like and don't like and what they wish would happen. But what they don't always see is the problem with dysfunction and poor leadership. Boundaries get skewed and the whole system becomes a mess. Problem solvers have to be very good at seeing the core issue and to not pass blame while they are assessing who is at fault. There really are perpetrators and victims and all conflicts should not be weighed as 50/50 at fault. The 50/50 distributional equation is typically performed by people who don't actually want to deal with or manage the real problem and assign responsibility like this so their minds don't have to perform the intellectual work of solving the real problem.

No matter who or what assigns responsibility to a problem, it is still important to find your own resolution as to how to handle it. Passing blame in a conflict only means you have yet to reach the true level of awareness. Avoiding blame can create a conflict because someone is always responsible for starting it. However, someone may start a conflict and the person who receives the blow may feel justified in making a war out of it. Understanding conflict can be very complex. Sometimes it is your passive response to abusive energy that perpetuates mistreatment.

Knowing how to move through conflict in life is a skill. It is one we should all have if we wish to see our purpose through. Knowing how to effectively resolve conflict protects you. It is like the brave self within that stands up for you.

Knowing resourceful ways to resolve conflict isn't easy. You are learning. This is all part of the journey. So many people think that solving a conflict means resolving it and that means making everyone work together harmoniously. This is not true. Many times conflict resolution is in solving what does not work for you so that you can remain more connected to your authentic truth. Learning to stay away from emotionally conflicted situations can diffuse problems that may trigger unhappiness in you. Sometimes avoiding conflicting situations makes things worse, too. One has to ask themselves if avoidance is creating a bigger problem than confronting it?

When you can move away from a place of peace rather than fear, then you know you have your power about you. You are not just avoiding or running from anything that life brings you. Finding and maintaining your power is what will give way to the real peace inside of you. The longer we run from a problem the longer time it takes just to turn and face it. Running gives the other portion of the conflict time to claim stake. There are many ways to resolve irreconcilable differences. Some people part ways and act as though there is no problem. Then there are people who really take the time required to forge understanding. These are usually the people who value peace and connection. You may have to attempt many different approaches before the conflict has a resolution. But eventually you will find it.

Just remain persistent. There is something this conflict is there to teach you. Ultimately, all you have to do is learn it.

The most empowered people are able to observe the truth of each person without having to judge or put down another person. They can see the moral values of right or wrong and choose to separate when values don't line up. They accept what is rather than trying to change the other person. However, they still set boundaries that physically, mentally and emotionally protect them.

The problem with expecting children to resolve conflict is they have no skill set to reinforce their boundaries and very few communication skills to effectively resolve it. The problem with expecting yourself to resolve a conflict comes from asking yourself Their behavior is their best defense in protecting their true selves from intrusions during their development. Poor behavior is actually coping behavior that is protecting the core self. Unfortunately, when parents don't understand how to interpret behavior, they may reprimand their kids for the slightest things. The very things the behavior is attempting to unconsciously protect themselves from become behaviors they are guilt and shamed for. This creates huge barriers to accessing the true self that hopefully people can work out later in life through the right approach.

One of the best therapists in working through guilt and shame is, Dave Jetson. He has a unique approach for *living true*. He guides individuals to their own truth in what he calls, Intuitive Experiential Workshops™. These workshops take place all over the U.S. and often times in other countries. More information is available through LivingTrueInc.com. His work has proven most beneficial to many people who have suffered various boundary violations.

The behavioral conditioning of people living out of congruency with their truth is what leads to self-inflicted and social violence. If the *Self* does not have a voice, it will act it out unconsciously whatever is taking place inside within it. The truth of the real self can look like anything. Truth is always love. Anything less than loving expression is an indication the true self has been separated. If the behavior can voice cannot protect itself it will shut down in anger, fear or sadness. It is very important to hear the underlying feelings that coincide with your actions.

To understand conflicts, we have to understand value systems. When people have different value systems conflicts always have a way of rising up. Not all parents value children. Not all children value parents. Not all personalities value other personalities. This creates a conflict in perception. Disagreements don't have to be constantly consuming your emotional life. When people can seek to understand the other person and yourself then you can learn to coexist without having to always fight. We have to honor a child even if they appear to have an undeveloped sense of self. Because if we don't honor them while they are developing, they will grow up with a very exaggerated sense of their false self. If they are living in their false self they can't find love. True self equals love, always. True self is never violating. Not to itself or another person. True self always seeks balance, always.

Value conflicts arise all of the time in relationships. Many people don't share the same values as to what is important to them. Choose to see the gift that this person brings in your life in the face of conflict without wanting to change them, then you have the ability to stand in your power and appreciate them. If you find that you just want to strangle them, inflict harm or, if a constant barrage of criticism is all that comes out, then you have yet to see the truth of this relationship. You have not yet received the full gift of what this person has come into your life to teach you if you still have anger at them. What people don't understand is when they hold the space for anger they hold the space for more conflict. This occurs because our natural evolution in life is towards love. The space for conflict increases to the point where we can't bear it anymore so we are forced to find love. That, or else die if we refuse to do so.

Responses of anger with the idea that peace is preferable, doesn't mean anger is bad. The degree of anger is always in the direct proportion of the violation. However, it is important to know what to do with your anger so that it doesn't make matters worse. When you receive the gift of what they were bringing, you cannot help but experience love from their presence and what it was teaching.

There is one caveat to this previous mentioned concept. There really are some very destructive people in this world that can and will take your life, whether it will be physical, psychological, or actual if you do not know how to protect yourself. There are several different types of anger that support you in certain times of crisis. That is why you have to follow your intuition when you work something out. When you are in this place within you that is much greater than your personality or your thoughts you can solve any problem with a higher thought. You are required to protect yourself.

Working to see the truth of any relationship is difficult because both people are holding onto their emotional truths and each one is different. Each one has a different perspective. Until each party reaches an expanded view and self-perspective, then there will always be a conflict of values to contend with.

THE JOURNEY INTO SELF UNDERSTANDING

Valerie Harper

5
Values

Values are part of the personality construct. They are reinforced by our family of origin. And they are unconsciously solidified into our psyche by the time we are seven. Values are the operating commands of life. The true self operates from very specific commands, much like the Christian Ten Commandments. The false self can operate from rules that deviate from this structured way of thinking. However, the truth is never clean cut so sometimes The Ten Commandments are not followed due to other aspects of the self.

When you are in the truth of the true self, following anything else will feel bad. The Ten Commandments become easy to follow when all aspects of the false self are healed. We cause a lot of religious damage by telling people they are bad instead of just observing things thy have to heal. The faulty rule is to say that if we follow The Ten Commandments then suddenly we are pure. This is untrue. Purity of self comes from having everything healed and congruent within you. Any religious guilt is only a sign of imbalance in those who persecute.

Following The Ten Commandments out of guilt and fear suddenly creates an inauthenticity because in God because only love is real. To deny the self is to deny God. But to give into false self is to deny God. So where does all of this lead?

There is a complex way of saying all things. The way of truth is the way to say all things in a simple truth—anything less than love is what we have to heal. Both the false self and true self have to be in alignment for the Ten Commandments to have full power. The false self must be given love, discipline and the right understanding for it to align with the true self for any congruency or healing. This is why we say healing from any addiction is a choice. The one who is healing has to be willing. It is in the willingness that something greater can come to us.

Values are commands within the self. The false self operates from a different set of commands than the true self. The false self operates from a bunch of rules and manmade concepts. Some of these rules are valuable. Some are not. Like the rule to pull someone over for doing 42 in 35 mile-an-hour zone for a $150 fee when they are not driving recklessly at all. What value does this rule give way to for the true self? Perhaps there is value. Perhaps there is no value at all?

The concept of being honest is a command that assumes someone knows the truth from a lie. There are many people who do not have a rational mind developed enough to determine whether or not what they are saying really happened or if they are just lying.

Negations of the truth have to do with what the mind is programmed to do. If we don't have the value of telling the truth programmed into our system, we will not honor or respect that value. We believe if people just "loved us enough" that they would do what we need them to do. This is not true. Many people are unaware of what they say, think and do or don't do.

Your value system is your operating system. It is your software for understanding and choosing. Without a value system you will say and do anything. It is within this value system that your choices and options flow through. You know you would never do something your value system wouldn't allow you to do. Then there are value systems that regard nothing as value. These are scary value systems that sometimes try to kill you or take what they can from your life. Different values are at the heart of any conflict.

Many people are losing the concept of *right and wrong* towards other human beings. These concepts are very simple but they are for some reason getting lost in what we are doing. In the face of fear, most people project their ideas and perceptions onto the other person. This means, whatever they *think* they are seeing is based on what they themselves are feeling. In other words, they have a feeling but don't know what to do with it, so they blame it on the other person for having it.

Projection is emotional confusion by putting it on the other person. People, especially adults, do this all of the time. They are out of touch with what they are really feeling. To make sense of their confused feelings they assume they know what they are seeing. This concept is complex. To learn more you can read books about psychology and psychological defense.

Many times we are perceiving something that isn't really even really an accurate interpretation of what we interpret it as. We project our fears, assumptions and foreknowledge in attempt to explain a situation. When our perceptions are based on fears and past conditionings, what we think we are seeing will always reflect what we were once experiencing—until the trauma of what happens gets healed.

The opposite also holds true. We can refuse to see something that *is* really happening and doubt the truth if we are conditioned to deny reality in order to make us feel safe. There are many people who prefer to live in their mental denials than be forced to see what is really taking place.

Anyone can confuse reality within their own mind. Seeing truth is a tricky process. It requires you to take actual events and make a scenario factual. The problem is, sometimes we don't actually see what is really happening so we miss factoring in actual events into our experience. The mind can deceive itself if it doesn't know what it is seeing or sensing. It takes practice and a willingness to discern how truth feels. This is only something that can be experienced, not taught through words.

Most people say things to themselves about what they see in a relationship that leave them feeling frustrated. We have these expectations of how we thing people "should" be and when they fail us we get angry with them. The truth is, we are all here doing our very best with what we know. It's just that some people have operating systems that have become confused, or sometimes called *dysfunctional*. Some minds are programmed with scary information.

Other minds are programmed with misinformation. Then there are minds that are well-rounded and harmonious. These minds allow for good health to emerge and beauty to be created all around them.

....

Many people are familiar with the concept that our mind is the center of our experiences. But few people have ever traversed the mind long enough to see where all of the thoughts actually come from. The thoughts and limiting perceptions come from our assumptions. We assume things about life based on our current ability to know things in the moment. This is how people end up regretting acts of violence. As time goes on, the defensive anger that committed the crime subsides and they are left to deal with the fateful consequences.

Even when we are not aware of what are mind is doing we are making assumptions. We are constantly prejudging and labeling everything. We are labeling everything and putting it into a category of good or bad depending on how we are emotionally feeling. We have to have some system for understanding. The problem is, if we don't have enough emotional awareness, we may throw good things out and overlook things that are destructive.

A well-trained mind has many faculties. It is first set up with a value system for optimal operating. These values include treating others with kindness and respect, as well as treating yourself with the same treatment. Other values also include be virtuous in your thoughts and words by focusing on thing that have meaning to you. Sometimes this means just disregarding other people's ill intent towards you.

Real values come from your core truth. They are designed to protect your core self from invasions that intending to harm you. Your values are really your terms for engagement. They were engineered in your mind based on how your family caregivers of early childhood environment operated. Making the quantum leap from what you were originally programmed with and replacing it with new values that come from truth can be an enormous undertaking. However, it can be done. It just requires the right coaching or training. There are many different schools of thought and religions that are designed to build the mind in a certain way. Falcons Guard is intended is one of them with the intention of building the sense of self to a point through self-discipline that you begin to create. Not just anything. But create from the truth of who you are in all things.

Core Values of Right & Wrong

It is okay to be angry at people.

It is okay to have a voice.

It is okay to ask for what you want and need.

It is okay to honor yourself.

It is okay to say "no" to people, places and certain things.

It is okay to experiment with new aspects of life.

It is okay to explore life as long as it doesn't hurt anybody.

If you hurt somebody, take responsibility. Do whatever you have to do to make the amends with somebody.

Live each life to the fullest.

Be good to your neighbors.

Treat others how you would like to be treated.

These are core values that might help you. The following are a list of core values that are incongruent with the true self. A value can also be in the form of what you should not do as well. For example:

Values that Are Not Okay

It is not okay to hurt somebody.

It is not okay to kill somebody.

It is not okay to take your anger out on others.

It is not okay to lie, to cheat and to steal.

It is not okay to lie and say you are going to do it and not do it. (This only reflects where you are not in your power.)

It is not okay to harm another person.

It is not okay to break agreements without clear understanding on the other persons part before you do it.

It is not okay to *not* earn your way in life.

It is not okay to inflict pain or suffering on another person.

It is not okay to hold a grudge.

It is not okay to acquiesce to someone else's demands.

It is not okay to be used or manipulated for someone else's benefit.

It is not okay to sit back and watch someone be abused and do nothing about it.

It is not okay to spend life playing video games. It develops nothing in the mind of quality.

It is not okay to hurt someone because they won't go out with you or rejected you.

It is not okay to sabotage another person's success just because they are currently more developed in a specific talent than you.

It is not okay to forge your signature on someone else's check.

It is not okay to steal money from another person.

It is not okay to skip out on your responsibilities or obligations.

It is not okay to have children and not care for them.

The gray areas in understanding these values is what you feel justified doing when someone does something to you. This is something to look at.

All of these aforementioned qualities are a list of sample value sets that can both help or hinder you. Inside, when you are focused on love, you will know the real truth of what to do. Always, follow the path of the most love. Follow these sample value systems for a while and see how powerful your inner self gets.

There is only one caveat to using these values— you must be with people who are similar to your value system. Otherwise, you can be as virtuous as you want and it won't get you anywhere within the social construct from which you are operating from. This is when it is important to remove yourself from these influences and or interaction. You have to ask yourself if it is really worth lowering your values just to get along with a social group that doesn't respect you, your boundaries, or honor where you are coming from. A clash in values is where all conflict comes from. It is up to you to find the most peaceful way of resolving that conflict. Feeling justified in responding poorly coincides with the old adage "two wrongs don't make a right." It feels terrible when someone doesn't honor who we are and it instigates a longstanding fight. The best thing to do is to find the place within where you have value. Cease to seek recognition from them knowing the person you are in conflict will most likely never validate you. Learn to love yourself. Know when to walk away and uphold your highest values so you can lead yourself into a better life.

When you understand the internal value system of yourself, you can see the kind of life you get. Of course there are always some gray areas. It is not always easy to navigate the waters of personal value systems. Many people have reinforced value systems from such a lack of love that they have no clue how to love. There are always exceptions to the rule when understanding what is the best behavior to choose. But when you stand in power rather than fear, you will find the right answer.

All psychological behavior makes sense when we know what fears, desires and skill set is driving it. Let go of the need to mindlessly react. Just set yourself up for good, solid responses. The best thing you can do when everyone is in conflict, is to stay calm, remain collected and just observe everyone's position within the situation. And when you have an emotional urge, apply it with the highest level of your own emotional intelligence. It is not worth lowering your EQ, your emotional quotient, to ruin your life with actions that are not right. The secret is to hold in your heart, the value of the one you are in conflict with, even when they have not the capacity of love to value you for who you are. You love them in the face of adversity and this is where you awaken to your real power that unlocks everything internally.

THE JOURNEY INTO SELF UNDERSTANDING

Valerie Harper

6
Family Roles

In each family there is a psychological role each person plays. If the family has not fully individuated with leading adults, the children that are born into the family will begin to play out certain, unexpected roles unconsciously. The reason for this is because a family operates as a unit. However, when the unit is dysfunctional, meaning its members are not in their power, each member can take on an alternate role rather than just participating in their own personal development.

A child will move from complete dependence, to independence and into interdependence naturally if their needs are taken care of at each stage along the way. Dependence is just as important as independence in certain stages. If development is missed because independence was forced at too early of an age, a person may become totally dependent in their older years as a result of unmet needs. We call this codependence.

Codependent roles are basically the undeveloped self reliant upon another person to take care of that person's *Self*. It is from this place of codependence that all sorts of things that can begin to happen. The violator may financially manipulate, control, abuse or extort the needy individual. The stronger personality is usually no stronger than the codependent individual that is usually perceived as weak. This dynamic is discussed in greater depth in my parenting book *Love & Strength*.

When we are codependent we look for anything to make us feel whole and safe because we don't have a solid internal foundation to give us this feeling of security. People can look to drugs, relationships and or people pleasing to soothe out of control feelings of insecurity. Whatever means is used to self-soothe is usually due to what the individual is predisposed to early on in life. If the concept of saying "no" to drugs wasn't there, the education that would guard against that choice won't be there either. We may become hyper-independent or helpless and needy. How the unmet emotional needs play out depends on the personality and what it did or didn't get during development.

We all have the potential to become extremely codependent if our emotional, mental and physical needs were not met when we were little. We have very specific emotional needs at different times of our development. When we are infants we need to be clothes, nurtured, dry and fed. When we are toddlers we need to be appropriately protected while we explore our world. When we are a little older we need to have a voice over what we do or do not want. That voice needs to be heard. When we get a little older we have social needs that need to be met, i.e., nice friends, people who care and a social support system that is fulfilling to interact with. Then we reach a point where we need to put all we have learned together and go out into the world and give life our very best attempt. Many of us fail miserably as we realize while we were developing we learned actually no real necessary life skills except for how to function within an emotional system that is so enmeshed it allowed for very little fun, very little ease or very little healthy interaction for positive development. We end up running scared, feeling alone and not wanting to live. When this happens it is the saddest thing because none of these feelings are the real truth about the self that has yet to develop.

When we want to die it is because we want the pain inside to leave us. We are so out of touch with our true personality, our true feelings, our true desires and our true yearnings that we just put it into one big overwhelming feeling of death. The truth is no matter how painful life gets, we all want to live. We all want to see our lives turn into something great. We just don't always know that we can. We don't have the tools or the methods. However, we can always learn how to lead ourselves into a great life no matter what our upbringing. We can change, learn to love ourselves and practice integrating new ways of developing as an adult to achieve a sense of personal self-mastery and integrate with heathier aspects of society.

In enmeshment, also known as emotional codependency, a child will not individuate because of how they are tied within a system of a family. There will be all sorts of power plays and consequences as you try to break free from the restriction. Knowing who you are, respecting yourself, respecting others for who they are, walking a path of love and non-violence and listening to your true self will give you the freedom you are looking for. Yes, it is easier to steal something you want from someone who you perceive to have more than you. However, nothing can ever be yours until you have taken the time to develop it within yourself first. You can attempt to take away someone else's happiness but in the long run, you will never be able to take away something you didn't earn or develop in yourself. We are all responsible for our own well-being. The faster we learn this the faster we can leave behind all suffering that mostly takes place within the mind. You can learn more about this in my book *Finding Home*.

……..

Your main purpose while developing is to learn enough social and interpersonal skills so you can individuate. The importance of individuating is so you can grow up, make your own choices and have your own life. Without individuation we remain limited and even trapped. The soul can't grow in these types of conditions. However, without proper guidance, individuation can be the scariest thing that could ever happen. This is why parents need to know how to love their children at all the different stages.

We see the fear of individuation fear being playing out in gangs and collective violence. This isn't power though like they think it is. This is the expression of their fears of individuation. They need to control enough people so they feel safer. This is dysfunction. This is an attempt to individuate without any guidance. The rebellion gives an emotional high that makes them feel like they are experiencing freedom. What they don't understand is how unintelligent they actually are both intellectually and emotionally and how they are harming other people. This doesn't matter to them because their true self is completely asleep. There are specific things people do o enforce this. And there are specific things people can do to awaken it.

To heal any type of violent behavior requires the person who is violent to tap into their real rage of never being cared for. The insults they received that they take out on other people all have to be felt and be consciously made aware of. The defenses required to breakthrough this wall of protection is astronomical, yet it can be done. The benefit is these individuals end up finding real freedom.

In breaking free of restriction, a form of controlled rebellion must occur in these situations. A person who is being abused has to find their power. Their anger is their power. But the anger must be kept in bounds. The anger has to be used for fuel for a greater good. It cannot harm another or the Self. If it does, it creates a karma that is tied to that person. The karmic debt is more painful than the damage inflicted. This is the game of life though. People don't see these threads because it happens at the deepest level.

Anger is a powerful force. Very few people have the power to let the anger pulse through their veins and do nothing about it except feel it. The most powerful person is one who can feel each ounce of their anger but take it out on no one. They don't have to suppress it, drink it away, shoot heroine to relieve it or direct it or do anything destructive with it. They are so powerful that all they have to do is *feel it*. They don't have to act on it or take it out on another person. They just sit with it and breathe through it.

Acted out violence is the number one cause for a self that wasn't taught respect or personal power. To manage this anger you must see where the person you are dealing with is out of their power. People who are in denial are easiest to control. The rage of a bully can be intimidating but you have more power when you see what they don't see. The same is true with the family members in an enmeshed family. They may not see what you know. They may not know how to love you or let you go. But this doesn't mean it is okay to take your anger out on them. It means quietly respecting them but holding your ground and making your way to your real power.

There are many different forms of violence. There is financial violence where you keep someone suppressed. There is physical violence as in getting beaten up. There is psychological violence that impacts mental health. There is sexual violence that penetrates the most primal and creative self. There is isolation or exclusion that leads to an underdeveloped sense of self. Breaking free of these forms of violence often times requires a system of healthy support.

An enmeshed family will act out violence on their family members and unconsciously keep them all stuck. These types of dynamics are intended to keep the family members powerless so they can't move on. Making changes in an emotional family structures can be incredibly difficult. It requires group participation and leaders that display balanced love and strength from the start. In order to break dysfunction, everyone must see their role and the part they play within the entire system.

To break free from dysfunctionality we must be able to dispel the emotional energy that has been built up and causing behaviors that are self-defeating. There is always a positive alternative for anything you are feeling. It is important to see the emotional self as two parts of energy. There is always a positive intent for what you are feeling. The feelings become destructive when you dispel that energy without intelligence emotionally.

Everyone has built up toxic emotionality. Some people have a little. Some people have a whole lot of toxic energy. Enmeshment keeps you stuck. Fear of moving forward keeps you stuck. Anything that isn't love keeps you stuck.

The key thing for you to recognize if you come from a family with enmeshed roles is to individuate as quickly as possible. Individuate by learning as many things as you can. If a constant conflict is presenting itself, just ignore it until you are strong enough to deal with it and then move on. Practice self-love. Read a lot of good material. Find people you resonate with and who care about you. Be around good people. Remain a good person. Be good to your family even if they do not know the things you know.

It is unfortunate that many people have to suffer. However, it is a reality. It helps us all grow. When you understand the emotional role you were fulfilling in the people who were emotionally empty, you will find the strength to individuate, start creating and emotionally let go.

Love is more powerful than fear, manpower or greed. The good of the light always beats out the darkness. The darkness takes its toll on the physical being but the spirit—which is only love—can override that power of what is fear. The physical being has to be capable of handling such energy. It is through our faith and convictions for what is love that we claim victory over what isn't love. This requires effort. The physical will must endure while the physical self undergoes transformation while never losing sight of who or what it is—pure love. When we observe the purpose of our challenges through this lens, it makes every challenge we go through, no matter how big or small, painful, but well worth it. Every challenge you face is an opportunity for you to remain connected or reconnect with your true self.

THE JOURNEY INTO SELF UNDERSTANDING

Valerie Harper

THE JOURNEY INTO SELF UNDERSTANDING

Valerie Harper

7

Behavior As Defense

To build the right psychology you must have self-understanding. Before you can ever have self-understanding you have to have a sense of who you are. The only way you will know who you are is if who you are is mirrored back to you. This means people respond to what you think, feel and display, accurately.

There are defense that keep you from internally processing life in such a way that prevent you from knowing who you are. Like a defensive driver, you have a defensive self. This self, if it feels unsafe, will act out. The psychological defenses intended to protect the core self are intended to defend against a reality the undeveloped mind is not yet ready to contend with. It takes inordinate amounts of strength to contend with certain problems we face in everyday life. These problems may include poverty, rejection, poor self-image, hunger and stress. People cope by using one or multiple of these defenses. More and more kids are going into these defenses due to premature exposure to things the mind is not yet psychologically prepared to handle. These defenses become part of frowned upon behavior.

The psychological defenses that present will depend on what you or another person is protecting themselves from. The mind will radically deny reality to manage anxiety from fearfully anticipated outcomes. The mind will develop this response to deny the fear of the unknown within the bodily system. Anxiety comes from the fear of what might about happening. It is trapped energy of fight or flight frozen. Even a healthy person will use this defenses at times of overwhelm. A person has to be skilled at talking themselves through fear.

Romantic relationships have a way of triggering the fearful responses of the self being over exposed through intimacy. We can deny reality if there is fear within the experience. In an intimate partnership you reveal who you are and see whether or not the other person accepts it. This can be terrifying to the false self. The false self is the social part of us that develops to gain approval in order to protect against rejection for survival.

Other defenses of the mind include: hyper self-evaluation, lies, cheating, aggression, emotionally shutting down, projections, denials, repression of true self, isolation, fear of other people, chronic disappointment, passive aggression and over intellectualizing everything. The way to correct and resolve the mental defenses that are intended to preserve the core self are to identify the challenges and learn to confront them, avoid them or neutralize them without compromising yourself. The next way is to always have a safe place where you can be. Even if you have no one in your life who cares about you now, you can be that safe place for yourself by telling yourself loving things. The next is just to observe these defenses and let them be. In time, with conscious knowledge, they can and will eventually heal with the right emotional release.

The best way to eliminate self-defeating behaviors is to accept yourself. Accept your feelings as emotional intelligence, but don't act on everything you feel you need to let out. Keep every emotion in bounds. Keep yourself always in check no matter how much will-power it takes. If you want to kill someone for taking away the only person you loved, keep yourself from doing that. Do not kill, do not harm, do not violate another person no matter what has happened. This is the most difficult emotion to contain because our minds can be underdeveloped. We are not to violate anyone even if they violated us. The laws of karma will take care of this. However, it is perfectly okay to stand up and even defend yourself. Just do so with emotional intelligence.

What does it mean to stand up for yourself through emotional intelligence? It means to defend and protect your divine providence without having to violate anyone else. Many people are asleep in life. They know not what they do. You, if you see it, are held more accountable. The more awake you are in your spirit, the more power. With more power comes greater responsibility. We know this line if we are familiar with modern superhero movies.

Your spirit is equipped with great power. You have to develop the self, first, before you can use it or even access it. To act out in violence is counterproductive.

Knowing the self is to manage the self. It takes more power to refrain from a negative act than to give into the fearful self and give into violence. Emotion is nothing than energy being produced from the personality and the distance between itself and what it wants to do. The power it takes to refrain from violent acts is the power you use to travel to the core of your true self. You can feel energy as power when you use it to cultivate higher thinking. When you operate this way, you are given the gift of intuition, which is to know, metaphorically, how to open emotional information and how to use it. This is nothing more than intuition—the power to know and sense something before it happens.

THE JOURNEY INTO SELF UNDERSTANDING

Valerie Harper

Intuition

You are equipped with all of the intuition that you need to navigate through life successfully. Having intuition doesn't mean that you have the intellectual knowledge to know how to do everything you want to do just yet. Intuition is the sixth-sense that protects you while you develop. Intuition is there for your survival but even still, the understanding for how to hear it has to fully understand it.

Intuition is developed first by tuning into your inner faculties. Some people are naturally more versed at the inner world than other people. They take the time to navigate their inner world and it shows. Intuition becomes highly developed when you listen to it.

There are five main ways of receiving intuitive messages. Again, to receive this guidance you must be tuned into the inner realms. One way is through seeing things in your mind's eye. You gain a sudden flash of something that you see but not in actual physical reality. Another way is through psychic hearing. You can actually hear the answer or intuitive guidance. Another way is through a sense or gut feeling. Your body moves you based on what it is sensing emotionally. Clairgognizance is just sheer knowing. You have a sense of what it is without even thinking. You just know it mentally and physically. There are other ways people receive intuitive hits but these ones are primary.

People develop their psychic abilities by listening internally to the messages they are seeing, sensing, tasting, feeling, smelling or observing. These qualities are developed more by what you are doing. If you are someone who feels things out, you will develop this intuitive ability more. If you are someone who thinks things out, you will develop this quality more. If you are someone who practices impulsive knowing than thinking fast intuitively will be developed.

Intuition helps us expand our experience. It helps keep us safe. And it also helps us be more creative. Intuition is the activity of the expanded self communicating with the smaller self. It doesn't always have something to say. However, you can always tune into it.

Sometimes we may feel our intuition has abandoned us because we experience something painful. Intuition doesn't prevent all painful things from happening. Sometimes we are meant to go through a certain experience in order to learn and grow spiritually. Listening to intuition can help you through the difficulty. It is what you fall back on when you, your small self, really isn't sure of something. Optimally, you will want to develop yourself on all levels so that you can deepen your intuition rather than rely on it solely.

Many people discount the mind due to popular theories that it blocks our progress. The intellect is amazing though at solving problems. It is important to relax the mind when following intuition. We have to quiet the chatter of the mind so we can hear it. When you find yourself in a difficult situation, the best thing you can do is get quiet. Center yourself in a place of peace and observe your thoughts. Once you unplug from your thoughts, tune into your intuition. Don't force intuition through over thinking. Just ask your higher self the question and be patient for what happens. The answers always come when you least expect it or have forgotten the problem.

It takes a lot of solid education to equip the mind with information for certain tasks. Intuition is a little different. It has to be more allowed. You can't program it. You have to gently work with it. Forcing it causes you to lose it. You have to allow it. Intuition is the sense that moves through you. It bypasses your intellect to guide you. Sometimes our minds do block us from acting on intuition because the mind can easily discount what is cannot see or have proof of. But it is also the mind that makes the choice to follow intuition, too. Without the intellect we are all fools. The mind is there to learn what intuitively comes through to support you.

As you begin to weigh intuitive understanding with some practical life concepts, you will begin to live a life that is richer and fuller with less effort. Your role as a teen is to prepare for adulthood. As you discover your truth from within, you develop a more refined intuition for taking action. Your intuition is the closest connection you have to your true self. You may not always understand it, but it is always guiding you to what your higher purpose.

·········

As a teen, you are about to enter a new realm of life called adulthood. This is when you will be required to have the inner mechanics and skills to know how to navigate your life experiences. The problem is most teens are focused on latest video games or hottest trends, not how to master the self or how to be a better humanitarian.

Most teens have big dreams for their lives. They think of where they would like to go and what resources they need to make life feel right. What they don't always see is how their choices and the choices people make around them impact everything. Some teens have yet to establish a good work ethic enough for self-discipline to even get them to where they want to be. They end up spending most of their adulthood dreaming about pie in the sky possibilities or contending with dysfunctional problems that strip their life of any real future possibilities.

We live in a world where people abdicate their power. What this means is they give up their personal power in order to keep the peace, look cool or avoid arguing. We also live in world where people stay in their power and are good to people. We live in a world of infinite possibilities. What you attract into your life has to do with the energetic experience of where you are at physically, mentally and emotionally. Where you are at is perfect actually. Each experience you have is contributing to the whole of what you are learning.

Just because there is a perfection in life, doesn't always mean life is perfect in situational ways. A lot of people are acting from their false self and creating a lot of problems. The good news is, life's evolution is always moving towards knowledge and healing. On a practical level though, there are things we must do to accomplish our goals, remain in this alignment and fulfill our purpose. These things include knowing who you are and honoring it. Letting others be as they are and reducing conflict. Learning how to navigate emotions and release the energy without holding the energy in or create a greater conflict. It is also about knowing how to follow your intuition and trusting it when you hear it. All of these things put you in a place of personal power. You can have this experience with or without loving parents. You can have a fulfilling life by taking the journey inward and developing these parts of yourself just by recognizing them.

There are problems we must overcome in order to remain healthy and alive. There are responsibilities we must learn to take care of or else we die. Learning to deal with these skills has to do with personal efficacy. The problem is, very few people actually know the Self they are actually protecting. This self is the real you. When you find it you enter your true power.

Very few people in the world know how to deal with someone who is in their power. Nor do they know how to walk in their power while honoring the power and free will of others. We are all fumbling about trying to understand what is happening. Some people belief life is about making the most money. Other people believe that life is about giving endlessly. Some people believe life is about one big problem they are solving while others believe it is their job to control everybody. Again, this comes from the origin of personalities. Be in the light side of your personality and there is harmony. Be in the shadow side and there is conflict.

Your real job in life is to be who you are, observe what is happening and find some way to contribute to this existence that is worth giving that is not porn, smut or life taking. Be someone in life that does something. Contribute something of value because you are value. Let go of your imbalanced tendencies and bring joy to the rest of the world around you. Sure, there is pain. You have probably gone through a lot of pain. There are probably people who have done some really mean things to you. This is not an attempt to diminish what happened to you. This is an attempt to say you are stronger than what happened to you. It is an encouragement to find the power within you that the people tried to take when they took out their wounds with their false self on you. This wasn't love. This was pain. Find the love in your life and create something amazing. Save it until you are safe. Preserve your most creative and precious things for people who can actually appreciate it and not just take it away. Live by values that support the real you.

To serve a greater purpose you must be in your power. To understand this concept one must be in their power. To feel comfortable with power *your* power you must be *in* your power. In order to be in your power you must understand your choices. When people don't know why they choose what they choose, they are operating from blind power. Your choice is your power. What you choose determines where you place your power.

We live in a world where people make choices every day that impact the lives of others without actually noticing or caring. We live amongst individuals that allow others to dictate their choices because they do not yet have the self-awareness that is required to decide for themselves whether or not they are going to acquiesce and buy into that power. People abdicate their power to another anytime they don't think for themselves.

They are instead operating from purely reactive emotion and when they are not self-aware. This is why taking the journey into self-awareness is so powerful. It illuminates all of the intentions behind your choices and gives you the power.

On a global level of power, there has been so much attention and focus on improving certain things that people are not even aware of what some of these choices are doing to other things such as our health, families and economy. Sometimes too much focus isn't a good thing. You will want to achieve a balance with how you manage your energy. You will want to be mindful of your power but not over fixate on it. You will want to be mindful of other people's emotional energies but still have your freedom. You will also want to be mindful of where you are investing your emotional energy; into what things are you focused on. Whatever has your power owns you. Make sure you remain close to your heart and continually seek the truth. Don't abdicate your power just because someone intimidates you. Make room for all personalities but set clear boundaries when they attempt to overpower you.

No matter what problem you face, all is always well. Tell the truth to yourself. Be honest with yourself about who you are and be honest with yourself about what you are seeing, sensing and feeling outside of you. Know your feelings, thoughts and faculties cannot deceive you if you are just honest about what they are picking up on instead of applying your own interpretation before you have the full truth. Don't let your mind deceive you just to feel better in the moment. Don't let yourself dip into drugs to find relief. Endure the experiences while solving the equation as to how to resolve the conflict. You are strong. You can do it. The combination of problems you face are training you well. You have a certain set of difficulties for a reason. It takes courage and personal power to resolve the dilemmas. You can do it though. Through good communication, keen observation and a well-intended heart, you can make it through anything. Trust the process. Trust what you are intuiting.

You are a teen which means you are in the second phase of your life. If you play your cards right, you might make it to age 99. You have to care for yourself physically, mentally and emotionally. This means you have to be mindful of the things you expose yourself to and what types of foods or chemicals you put in your body. Be mindful of the people you hang out with. Their energy can be pleasurable or catastrophic. Always follow your heart. And while you may not know or care to understand these problems you are facing, some of them may be interesting later on for what your overall life experience that is up and coming. In the future there will be some very specific situations you will be navigating that these experiences will help you.

THE JOURNEY INTO SELF UNDERSTANDING

Valerie Harper

Conclusion

This is a book was intended to prepare you on a new journey, not just for yourself, but for how you will be working together with humanity. The journey into adulthood is one that assumes more and more responsibility. Life is not just about sitting back and waiting for the latest technology or cute person to come in and start dating. There is real work to be done and just because you are a teen and you think you have your entire life ahead of you, doesn't mean you should be waiting. Take risks. Have fun. Assert yourself in new ways. Challenge yourself by taking one daily calculated risk that you could benefit from.

Life is meant to be lived, savored, challenged and after your work is done, sit back and take in the glory of the good you have created. Some people grow up and never assume any more responsibility. People who are responsible are powerful. They enjoy utilizing their personal power to keep things aligned properly. Responsibility means doing what you love and being in joy.

The older you get the more important it is to take the inner journey. Don't wait until you are on your death bed to heal relationships or find meaning. Do it now. There is no time like the present. The power is within you. All you have to do is grab it. You might fumble a little bit or look awkward. It doesn't matter. This life is your challenge.

You and your relationship with your inner self are always working on maintaining balance intellectually, physically, emotionally and financially. Because money is a physical extension of power, it must be used wisely. People who give the power away to people who use it destructively, gain more power collectively. Only good can triumph ultimately. When you take the journey inward you see the divine perfection in everything.

In the end, it is how much you honored life that counts. Love yourself, love others and have a great experience. But be mindful of deceptive forms of love that require you to discern truth rather than go into denial. Only a heart that is truly awakened can learn to love all things. This is a journey. Be mindful of the path you are on. Make the most of it by following your passions.

You can have a good life no matter what you are going through. The benefits of coming to know the real you is that you always know what to do. Your real self has guidance to offer you. You can rely on other people's input to tell you what to do and which way to go, but this isn't always helpful. Everyone has had a different set of circumstances their advice doesn't always align to what you need to know. In order to have a life that is successful you have to know who you are. It is through love that you come to know this power.

THE JOURNEY INTO SELF UNDERSTANDING

Valerie Harper

Workbook Section 1

Leading Yourself Into a Great Life

~~He who dies with the most toys wins.~~

He who dies revealing most of his/her real self—wins.

What are your thoughts when you read the above statements?

What are your beliefs that define your life purpose? Why do you believe you are here?

What would you like to see have take place in your life while you are here?

What are some things you really fear? What are some of the most terrorizing thoughts of what you could experience?

How might you begin to see your spirit as strong enough to endure anything?

What is your greatest purpose for learning? What area of life are you most driven to understand? Is it history? Politics? Relationships? Parenting? What area of life are you most drawn to and why do you think this is?

How might you prepare yourself for a great life knowing that you have this knowledge for your passions? How might you continue to support yourself physically, mentally and emotionally in ways that you can begin to see fulfillment in these areas begin to happen?

What areas of study would support your passions?

How much time are you willing to devote to your personal development?

What would your ideal plan of personal development look like? For example: "Workout 50 minutes a week, study daily, keep my word and start dating someone who is more like me."

What is the current framework of your life and how does it support what you are doing?

What types of problems do you have to deal with?

What fears rise up when you think about it?

What are your thoughts mostly focused on? What do you think about most often?

If you know thoughts have the power to create your life, what would you rather be focusing on?

How do you deal with conflict? Wat do your actions usually produce?

What personality type are you based on the section in the book that takes about this?

What personality types do you find yourself having to deal with?

What personality type are your caregiver?

How do you harmonize or clash with your caregivers personality type?

In terms of living in your true self verses false self, and the nature of your personality, how authentic would you say you feel you can be?

What authenticities do you hide about yourself in order to avoid conflict?

How might you begin to bring out more of who you are in all of your relationships?

What type of conflict do you anticipate might arise by bringing out more of who you are instead of trying to change yourself or the situation?

How might you lovingly handle the conflict?

When you are in a place of peace, how do you like to use your mind? Where do you like to place your focus and attention?

When you are in a place of fear, anger or frustration, where do you place your focus?

What do you wish you could destroy or get rid of when you are feeling terrible?

How might you consciously work through this emotional conflict rather than resorting to violence?

When you are feeling happy and positive, what do you love most about your life?

When you feel unhappy and like everything is going wrong, what is your perception? What are your judgements?

In the book it discusses how relationships are easily a source of conflict. Relationships can also be a source of great love. When you think about all of your relationships, which relationships are the easiest and which ones are the most difficult?

What is your definition of love in relationships?

What makes a mother loving?

What makes a father loving?

What makes a sibling worth having?

What are the greatest gifts you receive from your siblings?

What are the greatest challenges do you get to work through based on your siblings personalities?

If you could have any family dynamic of your choosing, how would each member in your family behave, respond and love you in a way that would be fulfilling?

Now, describe your family as they really are without any wishful thinking or imagining. How might you begin to see the perfection in this family dynamic without having to deny the truth of anything?

What would you say the gift is in what you are learning? What would you say the challenge is that may or may not be life sustaining? For example: a sibling that introduces you to drugs is a family system that is life threatening. What challenges will you have to overcome in order to get to the life you could only dream of having?

Many people's dreams come true without ever expecting them to. This is because there is an innate wisdom that is always guiding you. We know this system to be referred to as *intuition*. If you were to trust and follow your inner guidance system of intuition over listening to all the external commands of life, what do you think would happen?

If you were to assess what type of intuition you have, what would you say is the sense you hear your spirit speaking to you mostly? Is it through gut feelings and physical sensations? Is it through clear hearing that you receive your guidance? Is it through your gustatory sense, through flavors or sense of smell? Or, is it through clear visioning that you see in your mind's eye what is about to happen? Describe a scenario for each faculty for when your intuition came through and gave you feedback about something there was no other way you could know. It was just pure intuition...

Continue to describe the scenarios you have had with your intuition…

How do you wish you could use intuition? If you could know anything, anything at all, what would you like to know?

If you could have your life anyway you wanted, and you know that your intuition could get you there, would you be willing to follow your intuitions each and every directive no matter what?

What is your greatest fear to this type of blind faith and trust?

What is it you mind needs first before you can comfortably left go?

What is your greatest fear of having what happen in trusting your intuition no matter what?

Many of us do not like to be told "no"/ Intuition will sometimes tell us "no". Describe a time when you override your intuition and chose something else. How did it go?

If you could take away your problems and solve any conflict, which one would you first be resolving?

What problem would you solve after that?

And after that problem which one would come next?

How can you begin to use you intuition to navigate what happens next? What do you recognize as the core conflict?

Sometime sit is frustrating to work with intuition if we do not know ourselves well yet. It takes a lot of practice to hear the higher self. Start by observing first and just notice how it all connected. All of these suggestions and guidance are valid and possible when you have cleared away the rubble blocking your true self. Intuition comes from having a clear sense of peace inside of yourself. If at first you don't connect with your intuition, practice stilling your thoughts and letting go. It is difficult to trust and let go. But it is the only way to enter this part of yourself.

Can you ask your intuitive self what you might be doing that is contributing to the overall problem within the conflict?

What could you do, or not to, to resolve your portion of the conflict?

Workbook Section 2
Life Assessments

THE JOURNEY INTO SELF UNDERSTANDING

Describe your life...

If you were to describe your entire life with one theme, what would you say your life has been about?

If you were to see yourself as a character playing the main role in your life, how have you been acting?

If you could let go of the past and start living again, what would you release?

If you were to take responsibility in your part in the problem, what would you see you have been creating?

What do you do to cover up your true self in order to avoid what I uncomfortable?

How do you live your life each day? And is this the way you wish to be living?

How would you rather be living your life each day? What would you be doing?

How do these desired activities contribute to the good of the whole to your life and to the rest of humanity?

What one thing could you eliminate from your entire day that would make everything in and about your day even better?

When you think about who you are, do you feel you know who you are clearly?

What questions could you ask about yourself to understand yourself more thoroughly?

You can use the following questions to begin opening up to more understanding about who you are based on things that may be fairly easy understandings.

What are your dreams?

What are your favorite foods?

What is your favorite thing about life?

What is your favorite color?

What is your favorite shape?

What is your favorite subject?

What do you want to know?

What do you wish you would learn?

THE JOURNEY INTO SELF UNDERSTANDING

Who do you wish you could be?

What is your favorite kind of person?

Are you more motivated by power, love, beauty, kindness, relationships, status or positive energy? Then write about what you think of each quality.

In what other ways could you come to know yourself even more?

If you were to create your dream life, what would you have in it?

If you were to meet anyone you could, who would it be, and what topic would you wish to discuss with them?

If you were to look in the mirror and see your own beauty, what would you want to say to the person you see looking back at you?

If you were able to know the self that you don't already know, what would you hope to find out about this person?

The people who don't know how to connect to another through empathy are people who have never taken to develop an inner life that would allow for this type of relating. How could you show more compassion and empathy to those around you to make this place more loving?

THE JOURNEY INTO SELF UNDERSTANDING

Valerie Harper

Workbook Notes for EQ Lesson Plans 1-10

There are many different methods to use this next section. The following pages are blank so each page will be a guided lesson by an instructor. If you do not have an instructor for this section, you may use this section as a journal.

Lesson 1

Lesson 2

Lesson 3

Lesson 4

Lesson 5

Lesson 6

Lesson 7

Lesson 8

Lesson 9

Lesson 10

Notes

Notes

Notes

20 Principles for a Great Life

1. Respect yourself
2. Respect your Parents
3. Respect your Intuition
4. Respect everyone's nature
5. Learn to love who you are.
6. Strive to know your nature.
7. Live your best self.
8. Trust your intuition to lead you into greatness.
9. Let go of fears and learn to live with non-violence.
10. Recognize emotion for energy. It is what you do with this energy that determines if it becomes positive or negative.
11. Transmute all frustrations into self-awareness.
12. Use all challenges as fuel to get to the real, core conflict.
13. Resolve all conflicts through truth and empowerment, not force or manipulation.
14. Seek to see the beauty in all of life while recognizing divine perfection.
15. Trust innate wisdom knowing that everyday you will receive a new life lesson and that your actions will be different.
16. Know that you can always grow. It doesn't matter where you have come from. You are always free to be your greatness.
17. Use education for personal development.
18. Remember intellectual intelligence without emotional intelligence means nothing.
19. Act with love and see your higher beauty.
20. Forgive those around you who have harmed you, after you have claimed victory over your personal emppowerment.

Falcons Guards Books are a trademark of a Mountain Lotus Publications Collection. For more information on upcoming classes and events, please visit our website at MountainLotusPublications.com.

For more information about Falcons Guard Centers or to make a contribution to the troubled and homeless youth in this country, please visit FalconsGuardCenter.org.

About the Author

Valerie Harper is a mother of two, a business entrepreneur, and leader in emotional intelligence. She has authored over 32 books on subjects relating to human development, all of which are available through Mountain Lotus Publications, a publishing company that focuses on psychology, science and tacit knowledge.

Her books are also available through Amazon, Kindle and MountainLotusPublications.com. She conducts workshops and trainings in locations throughout the U.S.. These include both educational trainings for professional development and facilitator trainings for parenting and personal development.

Valerie's private consulting firm, Valerie Harper Consulting and True Wealth Consulting, is located in Scottsdale, Arizona, where she resides. He work focuses on personal development, business development, talent development as well as children and families.

For information on her consulting service, or regarding her availability for keynote lectures, teaching courses or developing greater emotional intelligence, Valerie can be contacted through her website, ValerieHarperConsulting.com, or by email at valerieharperconsulting@gmail.com.

www.ingramcontent.com/pod-product-compliance
Lightning Source LLC
Chambersburg PA
CBHW051928160426
43198CB00012B/2079